WHY YOU MUST LISTEN TO THE ADVISES OF YOUR MOTHER

Victor Cosmas

CONTENTS

FOREWORD

Studies show that sometimes around the age of ten or eleven, children begin to experience hormonal shifts in their body resulting to puberty.

These shifts often lead to emotional outbursts, unexpected stubborn behaviour and sometimes withdrawal and feelings of maturity.

At this point in time, they may be very difficult to control or adhere to instructions.

However, this book talks a lot about the characteristics and skilful nature of a mother that tells the reader why it is important to listen to his or her mother thereby correcting or reducing disobedience and misbehaviour.

I therefore recommend this book to all children particularly those who are about turning the age of eighteen and above.

Arla George,

Retired Doctor
University Hospital of Hartlepool
United Kingdom.

PREFACE

This book is a non-fiction book that contains impactful messages, few quotes, few life lessons and natures of a mother that will make you have a rethink on why you must listen to your mother no matter the age, maturity or education you have attained; in case no one has ever told you.

INTRODUCTION

I write this book to let you know that there are some things you will never understand or get to know better until you reach some certain age.

Growing up as a child during my teen-age, i was so stubborn and never listened to my mother. I thought i knew it all and just wanted to explore live and do anything without her consent but at the end of it all, i learnt things the hard way and made a lot of mistakes in live; some i have not been able to forgive myself even till today.

This book contains few reasons why you should listen to your mother coupled with few of my life experiences and that of a late neighbourhood friend of mine who go by the name Linda. As you go through this book, i hope you learn from it and have an understanding of what i am talking about.

CHAPTER 1 WHO IS A MOTHER

Sometimes, mothers can be so annoying especially when she gives you an instruction or advises you on something you literally never wanted to do.

But she is not just a mere woman that birthed you; but someone who is attached to you right from the beginning of your life cycle. Starting from her womb (umbilical cord) up till the time you were born.

Just as the popular poem by Ann Taylor goes (Who sat and watch my infant head when sleeping on my cradle bed, and tears of sweet affection shed my mother...

When pain and sickness made me cry, who gazed upon my heavy eye, and wept for fear that I should die..., my mother...

Who taught my infant lips to pray and love Gods holy book and day and to walk in pleasant way..., my mother...

And can I ever cease to be affectionate and kind to thee, who was so very kind to me..., my mother...

Ah no! the thought I cannot bear, and if God please my life to spear I hope I shall reward the care..., my mother...

When thou art feeble, old and grey, my health and arm shall be thy stay, ans I will soothe thy pains away, my mother....) e.t.c...

As the poem goes, you can see that your mother is attached to you emotionally, psychologically, physically, and otherwise. She is your first love before anyone else. She loves you unconditionally regardless of how tall; short, fat, slim, beautiful or ugly you may appear. So always pay attention to her.

CHAPTER 2 RARE QUALITIES OF A MOTHER

A mother is your guardian

Your lovely mother brought you into this world by birth therefore, she has that burning passion to lead you and to guide you towards the right path and also to help you in achieving greatness.

THEY CAN STAKE THEIR NECK FOR YOU

ALL caring mother has that natural protective desire when it comes to their children because of the love they have for them. They love and cherish you unconditionally and would not want to see you get hurt.

This implies that if it means risking their lives to save yours, then they will surely do it.

THEY KNOW YOU BETTER THAN ANYONE

Growing up, at the age of sixteen about entering college, my mother and I had a discussion about choosing a program to study at the university. I told her I wanted to study electrical engineering. She said I knew you would choose Electrical Engineering as your choice program and that i was going to be a lover of dogs so i asked her how she knew; she said she bought a lot of toys for me growing up and among all the toys, the ones that i love most was the electronic devices and the teddy dog and i usually loose whatever electronic device i lay my hands on.

So you see, mothers know a lot about us especially our strength, our weakness, our bad sides and our good sides because they were the ones taking care of us, studying us, watching and observing us as we grow.

THEY LOVE TO SEE YOUR PROGRESS

Every mother derives joy in the success and accomplishment of their children. I tell you most solemnly, there is no one in this world that derives pleasure in your success more than your mother.

Your friends, or siblings may get jealous or become envious of you as you excel or succeed in live but your mother will never be. Instead, she will always pray for you and support you at all times.

THEY CAN SACRIFICE THEIR
LAST FOR YOU

There are only few people in the world who could sacrifice their last penny or any form of assistance to you when ever it's needed. Your mother is the only woman that can do that without even thinking about it. I have lost count on the number of times she assisted me with loans. Loans I collected without even paying interest or paying back. So that's just a mother for you.

THEY WILL ALWAYS BE THERE FOR YOU

Your caring mother will always be there for you no matter what. They will always have your back. If you by any chance go astray or offend your mother i would strongly advise you to kindly go back and apologize to her. She would surely hear you out and accept you back.

CHAPTER 3 WHY MUST YOU LISTEN TO YOUR MOTHER

She is always, looking out for you

Your lovey mother is always looking out for you like a guardian angel right from when you were a baby. she is always on the lookout for you because of that natural love, emotional and psychological connection she has with you. You may not want to agree with me but the fact still remains that mothers, always think of us almost all the time. Sometimes, they get worried sick especially when we go missing. Your health and safety is their number one priority. So try and listen to your mum whenever she talks. Growing up at the age of thirteen, in a ghetto-like community, i played a lot especially during late hours. I was very passionate about football. I can play football from morning till evening without feeling hungry or tired.

Until one faithful day, as i was about entering the house after playing outside; an insect entered my ear. I still remember it was my right ear. It was so terrific and horrifying. I was so scared and began to cry. As a child, i did everything to get it out but I couldn't. All i could hear was the buzzling and the movement of the insect inside my ear. I was so scared and thought i was going to go deaf. It was late evening and the environment was very dark. Before this, my mother used to caution me to avoid staying out late in the evenings. She used to caution me that *"it's not good to stay outside at night that a lot of bad things happen during late hours"* but i never listened to her. Every day, she would yell, scold and warn me about it; but did I listen? No! Luckily for me, i ran home immediately crying to my mother, "Mummy! Mummy! Something is inside my ear." I was yelling and crying as i moved towards her. She scolded me for a while then held me closer and looked into my ear but she saw nothing. She then quickly rushed me into the nearest clinic where i was administered by a nurse who poured an amount of water into that particular ear facing upward and after sometime, the water got into my ear she then faced my ear downwards and the little insect came out alive together with the water and fell on the floor. And then it was killed. That was how i regained my freedom and since then, I never stayed out late night ever again. Can you imagine if the insect had bitten my ear drum?

May be i would have gone deaf forever?
But thank God I was saved by the nurse.

THEY HAVE GONE THROUGH
MANY LIFE EXPERIENCES

Most mothers have gone through much life experience; A life experience is any good or bad event that happened to you and changes your way of behaviour. There are two life experiences that have changed my behaviour. first, was the story I mentioned about an insect getting into my ear, it's a life experience that has made me to avoid late night because anytime i remember that event, i will quickly rush home whenever it's getting dark because i wouldn't want any insect to get into my ears again or something worse to happen to me.

Secondly was taking excess amount of sugar. I love sweet foods so much that i can't do without having them. My cravings for sweet food can't be compared to none. If an award was to be given to those that love eating sweet food in my community, then i would have won the best award.

However, my mother advised that *"taking sugar is good but taking excessive sugar content is no good for the health*". But as a child then, I was so stubborn and never listened. No matter how she tries to hide sweet foods from me to curtail my consumption, i will always have my way around. At the end of the day, it affected my health. I became obese. I gained so much weight that i was so ashamed to interact with people in my community until i disciplined my body. I was enrolled into the Gym; i did a lot of exercise and took various weight-loss therapies before i finally regained my shape. It was a difficult experience that taught me how to curtail my consumption for sweet food.

Likewise, most mothers have gone through many live experiences more than we do because they have lived ahead of us. You have to remember that your mother was once a baby before she became a mother. She didn't just fall down from the sky. She learnt a lot of things during her childhood. Some of the things she learnt were taught to her by her own mother, from professional individuals or guardian, books, family members, or from the internet. She must have seen people around her such as her siblings, uncles, aunties and neighbours gone through mistakes and various worse life experiences. And that is why whenever she advises you or talks to you, she talks not only because she loves you but because she does not want you to get hurt by passing through those worse experiences. Therefore always pay attention to her.

It has been scientifically proven that most mothers are wiser and have a way of seeing things before anyone else does. This is because wisdom comes with age and they are older than we are. Also they make use of their sixth sense(a high level of instinct or intuitions) that enables them judge things or know things that other people do not know. For example, when you make a new friend, your friend may seem all loving, nice, caring and funny, you guys get along very well, and you've decided you're best friends. But when your friend stops by your house and greets your mother, your mother picks up on a whole different vibe. Of course, you don't see it and you argue with her, but somehow, our mothers are always right. Once that wonderful friend of yours starts showing their bad side and stabs you at the back that is when you would realize that once again, you should have listened to your mother.

Please permit me at this juncture to tell you a

summary about my late neighbourhood friend Linda. Linda was a good girl all loving, nice and caring; she stood at exactly five feet, two inch tall. She was very beautiful and dark in complexion. We grew up in the same High School. She was my best friend in High school. We sat together and do almost everything together in high school. She was so brilliant and intelligent. I could remember when she told me that she wants to be a doctor when she grow up. But her behaviour and disobedience started when she began following bad friends in our community. Her mother warned her to stay away from them but she never listened. Although her mother was not always home all the time. She goes to work every morning and comes back home in the evening. Her mother was a single parent. Linda never listened to her mother because she enjoyed the company of her friends as they were the only ones that keep her busy in the community when her mother goes to work. She never knew that *"bad company corrupts good behaviour"*. I also as a kid noticed some of her bad excesses and tried to talk some senses into her but she never listened. We only do our group work and class assignments together and that was all. All of a sudden, she started portraying bad characters like being disrespectful, rude and all of that. I normally visit her in her house whenever school was on holidays. There was a day during one of the holidays I paid her a visit; and to my greatest surprise, i met her in the company of some bad friends (boys and girls) smoking, chatting and laughing. She was around age seventeen then. She learnt smoking, alcohol and lots of bad stuffs from her friends. She would normally sneak out at night to attend all manner of party without her mother's consent. The worst thing that happened to her was when she began taking drugs and cocaine. She became addicted to drugs, cocaine and Prostitution. Her mother tried at all cost to guide her and to put her in order but she was so stubborn and never listened. At the end of it all, she contracted HIV and all manner of illness. Her caring mother even took her to a rehabilitation hospital due to the effect of the drugs on her. She dropped out from school and then she became terribly ill and died. On her sick bed before she died, she cried and begged her mother to forgive her. She said if only she had listened, all of these wouldn't have happened.

Also, as one begins to grow old, a time would come when you fall in love or go out on a date.

However, when it's time to start dating or courting, i would strongly advise you listen to your mother because most mothers have a personality of the kind of boy or girl they want for their child when it comes to finding the right girlfriend or boyfriend and sometimes those standard or specification are higher than the ones that you have for yourself. And it seems that no matter whom you introduce to her, she would always find something wrong with him or her. Because of this, it's hard to believe her when she tells you this guy or this girl is no good for you. Whenever you invite him or her over for dinner to meet the family and she spends sometime interrogating him or her about family life and plans for the future, he or she may have been able to sweet talk you into getting what they wanted, but nothing gets past mum. With her sixth sense, she can perceive the right person for you. But of course, when you don't listen to her advice and end up dating the guy or lady only for you to find out something bad about them later, then you will remember that your mother was right the whole time. I have seen several occasions where things turned out bad for people as a result of not listening and heeding to their mothers advice. An uncle of mine who got married to the woman he was advised not to marry ended up regretting the marriage barely one year in marriage and right now, they are divorced.

Therefore, *"the words and advises of our mothers*

are words of wisdom. The wise one hears and gets wiser". I use to hear some kids who wants to get things done their way regardless of the outcome or danger and without advice or consent but the truth is that there is no joy when you learn by mistake. You could harm yourself or end your life in the process or not being able to forgive yourself. "*Your mother's advises and opinion are of good intention towards you and not of evil so always listen to her*". If you feel she does not understand, you can always ask questions to get the reason behind her opinion rather than arguing with her or opposing her.

Please young ones always listen to your mother because; it pays to listen to her.

ACKNOWLEDGEMENT

A big thank you to my biological mother whose love, advice, care and sacrifice has made me a better man that i am today.
It was the memories of all the advice she gave me during my childhood that inspired me to write this book.

ABOUT THE BOOK

Despite growing up in a Ghetto-like community where killings, drugs prostitution and violence where the order of the day; Victor Cosmas refused to be influenced by the happenings in his community where he grew up and still stood out to be a better person among all his peers as a result of listening and heeding to the advises that was given to him by his mother.

ABOUT THE AUTHOR

Victor Cosmas

Victor Cosmas is a graduate of Electrical and Electronic engineer; a teacher by profession and also a writer.

His love and passion towards children and a better society has motivated him towards writing books and stories that teaches good morals and values. He has taught and written a good number of books and stories that have benefitted a good number of children in his community;hence making his community a better place.